FLYING THE NORTH ATLANTIC

FLYING THE NORTH ATLANTIC

Jim Barry

B.T. Batsford Ltd, London

Typeset by Servis Filmsetting Ltd,
Manchester

Printed in Great Britain
by Anchor Brendon Ltd
Tiptree, Essex
for the publishers,
B.T. Batsford Ltd
4 Fitzhardinge Street
London
WIH oAH

Contents

Acknowledgements

The author and publishers thank the following for their help with this book:
Airlines: Air Canada; British Airways; Pan American; TWA. Airport Authorities: Aer Rianta/Irish Airports; British Airports Authority; The Port Authority of New York and New Jersey; Transport Canada. Manufacturers: Boeing Airplane Company; Lockheed Corporation International; McDonnell Douglas/Douglas Aircraft Corporation; Short Brothers plc; United Technologies/Sikorsky Aircraft. Miscellaneous: Canadian High Commission, London; Embassy of Iceland, London; Embassy of the United States, London; Ministry of Defence, London; New England Air Museum, Connecticut; Royal Air Force Museum, London.

Introduction:

Pre-war and wartime civil flying

The Irish connection

The Atlantic Ocean has fascinated and challenged man for centuries, and a variety of craft has travelled its waters since the first known voyage, in the sixth century, by St Brendan of Clonfert, from Ireland. Both the airships and the conventional aircraft saw the dawn of the next era in Atlantic travel, but the airship's role was brief and it was left to the heavier-than-air craft to blaze the trail.

The Irish connection was maintained through successful flights by conventional aircraft. The first ever direct flight across the Atlantic by Allcock and Brown ended in County Galway in the west of Ireland. The first successful westbound flight took off from Baldonnel Aerodrome, near Dublin, crewed by two German pilots, Baron von Hunefeld and Captain Koehl, with Commandant Fitzmaurice of the Irish Air Corps navigating the flight to Labrador. Although the first solo flight, by Colonel Lindbergh, was from New York non-stop to Paris, this famous pilot was later to exercise a strong influence on shaping the future of Irish aviation and, in turn, the development of the North Atlantic routes. It was not until the late 1930s that the airspace over the Atlantic Ocean was finally to be mastered sufficiently to operate scheduled transatlantic services and, true to tradition, Ireland was the eastern take-off point.

Selecting the Irish base

By 1934 the governments of Great Britain, America, Canada and Ireland joined in an agreement to cooperate in the establishment of regular transatlantic air services – Ireland would provide an international airport, catering for land planes and flying boats, and Canada would provide similar facilities in Newfoundland.

Colonel Lindbergh, on behalf of Pan American Airways, carried out an evaluation of possible Atlantic routes in 1933, and visited Ireland to examine proposed sites for a flying boat base. Later, he was part of a team of British and American experts who made a strong recommendation to the Irish Government to develop the site known as Rineanna, on the Clare side of the Shannon estuary and about 12 miles (19 km) west of Limerick City, as a combined land and marine airport. The recommendation was accepted, and work began on the base in 1936.

Owing to the mammoth task involved in turning Rineanna into a

1 Early airship Atlantic crossing –
On 29 July 1930 the airship R100 left
Cardington in Britain bound for
Montreal, commanded by Captain
R.S. Booth, the westbound crossing
taking 79 hours and the return to
Cardington 56½ hours. It is interesting
to note that 79 hours comes to 3.3 days
and a Concorde's Atlantic flying time
is in the region of 3.3 hours. The
R100 never flew again, because of a
tragic accident in which the R101
crashed into a hillside near Beauvais
in France in October 1930, bursting
into flames and leaving only six
survivors out of a total of 54 on board.

2 Pan American pioneers (facing page) – *Charles A. Lindbergh* (left) *and founder Juan Trippe, on the tarmac in Panama.*

3 A view of Foynes (above) – *Foynes, a seaport of long standing, was ideally suited as a flying boat base. There was a safe mooring area with two short channels leading to the open estuary. A new concrete jetty, with a floating landing stage, had been built a few years previously. The seaport had played host in the early years of the century to the Royal Navy, and later played host again to three international airlines.*

land plane and flying boat base (extensive dredging of marshy land being essential for a flying boat operation) it was found necessary to have an interim flying boat base, and the nearby port of Foynes was chosen. Foynes, on the County Limerick (southern) bank of the river Shannon, was only about 10 miles (16 km) from Rineanna, but unfortunately it would not be possible to link the bases by boat and, with the nearest bridge at Limerick City, the road distance was about 40 miles (64 km). This made life difficult in the near future when both bases (together to become known as Shannon Airport) had to work closely together.

The battle of the airlines

Without any doubt, the prime mover in the development of transatlantic air services was Pan American Airways, a tough pioneering company which had started in 1927. Under its dynamic president, Juan Trippe, Pan American rapidly built up a network of services, and a great deal of influence throughout the world.

At a conference on establishing mail and passenger services by air across the North Atlantic held at Ottawa in December 1935, it was decided that, in addition to Foynes, temporary airports would be made available for experimental and survey flying boat flights; these

4 Sikorsky 42 flying boat – Pan American's S42 flying boat NC1676 (Clipper III) carried out two Atlantic survey flights in 1937, in both cases commanded by Captain Harold Gray, and both flights were timed to coincide with Imperial Airway's first two survey flights. Pan American's routing for both flights was Port Washington (on Long Island, New York)/Shediac (New Brunswick)/Botwood (Newfoundland)/Foynes/Southampton, and return.

5 G-ADHM (Caledonia) – Two
Imperial Airways Short C class S23
flying boats were modified with long
range fuel tanks for survey flights on
the North Atlantic. With Captain
Wilcockson in command, the first
survey flight on 5 July 1937,
Caledonia, was routed
Southampton/Foynes/Botwood
(Newfoundland)/Montreal/New
York, and return. On 29 July, with
Captain Powell in command,

Caledonia *made a second survey*
flight over the same route.

6 *G-ADUV* **(Cambria)** *– Imperial Airways second modified C class flying boat, Cambria, with Captain Powell in command, was used over the same route for a third survey flight on 29 August 1937.*

These two Short C class S23s were modified for in-flight refuelling to enable Imperial Airways at least to provide regular Atlantic mail service to parallel the Pan American scheduled passenger service with the Boeing 314s (passengers were not allowed to travel on aircraft refuelled in-flight by airborne tankers). The two S23s were stripped of all furnishings and srengthened, with lighter and more economical Bristol engines installed, to increase their maximum usable take-off weight by 4536 kg (10,000 lb). They were re-designated S30s. The back-up flight refuelling tanker aircraft, converted Harrow bombers (landplanes), were based at Rineanna, Gander (Newfoundland) and Montreal.

Eight round trips, carrying mail, were completed by the two S30s, supported by the Harrow tankers. The first westbound flight started from Southampton on 5 August 1939 – Caribou, commanded by Captain Kelly-Rogers, routed via Foynes, Botwood, Montreal, to New York. The Harrow tanker which refuelled that first westbound flight of the series, after it became airborne from Foynes, was based at Rineanna, and piloted by Geoffrey Tyson, later well known as the test pilot of the postwar mammoth turbo-propeller flying boat, the Saunders-Roe Princess. Both Cabot and Caribou were transferred to the RAF after their Atlantic mail-carrying, in-flight-refuelled trips. Sadly, both were lost through enemy action in May 1940.

bases were to be at Botwood (Newfoundland), Shediac (New Brunswick) and Montreal; terminal airports would be at Southampton and at Port Washington (New York). The airlines concerned were Imperial Airways of the United Kingdom, and Pan American, of America. The governments represented at the conference were those of Britain, Canada, Newfoundland and Ireland. Pan American would operate reciprocal flying boat services with Imperial Airways. Thus a political framework was established for a flying boat operation, but soon there was friction between Pan American and the British Government. The American airline wished to go ahead with trial flights, using their Sikorsky 42 flying boats, but Imperial Airways had no suitable aircraft available and the British Government insisted that both airlines start simultaneously. By the end of 1936, Imperial Airways having available two Short C class Empire flying boats, modified with extra long range fuel tanks, both sides were working towards a series of survey flights.

Survey flights and proposed schedules

The survey flights were carried out during 1937, Pan American operating from New York via Shediac, Botwood and Foynes to Southampton (and back), and Imperial Airways operating from Southampton, via Foynes, Botwood and Montreal to New York (and back). For both airlines the critical legs were the journeys in both directions between Foynes and Botwood.

During 1938, a North Atlantic air route conference was held in Dublin, between the governments of Ireland, Great Britain, Canada and America, and representatives of Imperial Airways and Pan American. Detailed arrangements were made for proposed scheduled services, making full use of ground organization, meteorology and radio. From this conference emerged the Transatlantic Air Service Safety Organisation, subsequently known as TASSO, destined to play an essential part in commercial aviation.

Friction among Pan American and Imperial Airways, and the British Government continued over organizing the flying boat operation. Pan American knew what they wanted – the Boeing 314 flying boat was designed to meet their specifications and they had ordered six of these aircraft, with options on a further six. The first flight by a 314 was in June 1938, less than two years after they had signed the contract; all six aircraft were delivered between January and June 1939.

The Mercury-Mayo composite

At this time, Imperial Airways appeared more concerned with their Empire routes, for which Atlantic range was not needed, but nevertheless they returned to the Atlantic to experiment with the 'pick-a-back' concept. The 'pick-a-back' was two aircraft in one: the top aircraft broke away to continue the intended flight while the lower aircraft, or 'mother' ship, landed back at the departure point. Its invention was necessitated by Imperial Airways not having an aircraft with sufficient range to get airborne and fly the Atlantic with a

9 NC18605 (Dixie Clipper) – *The Boeing 314 flying boat was designed to meet the specification issued by Pan American in 1936 for a long range four engined flying boat. These aircraft introduced a new era of passenger comfort and operating dependability. The crew compartment was as big as the passenger cabin of a DC3, and the lower deck compartments offered a dining saloon and a self-contained suite in the rear. Berth sleeping accommodation was provided for all passengers. A tunnel in each wing gave access to the new Wright 'Double Cyclone' engines, by the flight engineers, in flight. The aircraft's fuel was carried in the enormous sponsons.*

NC
18605

10 Mercury-Mayo Composite – *The first payload (mail) to be carried across the Atlantic was achieved through using the Mercury-Mayo composite on the critical sector, Foynes/Botwood – based on the concept that an aircraft can fly with a greater load than it can lift! When airborne from Foynes, Mercury separated from the mother ship, Maia and flew on to Botwood under the command of Captain (later Air Vice-Marshal) D.C.T. Bennett, operating under its own power for the Botwood/Montreal and Montreal/New York sectors, and returning – also under its own power – via the Azores and Lisbon.*

11 A Pan Am 314 'clipper ship' –
Here the 314 is in wartime camouflage
with the American flag prominently
displayed.

payload (other than by using in-flight refuelling by an airborne tanker). This composite aircraft was developed as an alternative to in-flight refuelling. The top aircraft was a four engined sea-plane (with floats, as distinct from a flying boat, which has a hull), and the lower aircraft was a four engined flying boat – a modified Short C class.

Start of scheduled flights

1939 saw an intensification of proving flights and, most importantly, the delivery on 27 January by the Boeing Airplane Company to Pan American of their first 314 flying boat.

Both France and Great Britain had very experienced airmen, but neither had the right aircraft to mount scheduled services across the North Atlantic. Pan American also had very experienced airmen, and, in addition, they had the right aircraft in their newly acquired Boeing 314. They were not prepared to postpone scheduled flights any longer.

On 28 June 1939 a Pan American Airways (Pan Am) Boeing 314 flying boat landed at Shannon Airport, Foynes. NC18603, the *Yankee Clipper* had been routed from New York to Shediac (New Brunswick), Botwood (Newfoundland), Foynes, and then to its European terminal, Southampton. This first scheduled flight across the North Atlantic experienced en route weather problems – the sort of problems that were to cause much trouble for years to come, both to operators and to passengers. There were 11 crew, with Captain Gray (by now an Atlantic veteran) in command. Among the 18 passengers was Juan Trippe, Pan Am's famous founder-president. This was a big first for Boeing and Pan Am, and there would be many more firsts for both the airline and the manufacturer in the Atlantic story.

Pan Am's scheduled flights continued through the summer of 1939, using the same northern routing. During this period Imperial Airways continued survey flights, again using modified C class flying boats, providing reciprocal scheduled services carrying mail.

In July 1939 Pan Am produced the first transatlantic timetable, with flight numbers 100 eastbound and 101 westbound – flight numbers still used and well remembered as having been used for the 'President' (luxury, first class) flights which began after the war. The outbreak of war in September 1939 was to bring dramatic changes to both the marine and land plane bases at Shannon Airport. For a start, Pan Am's scheduled flights were temporarily discontinued.

BOAC and the start of wartime commercial flights

By early 1940 Imperial Airways had been renamed as British Overseas Airways Corporation (BOAC), an airline in dire need of aircraft with transatlantic capability. In addition to the six Boeing 314 flying boats already acquired, Pan Am had turned their option for a further six aircraft into a firm order, and these aircraft were now under construction. They were to be 314A models, with improved take-off weight, greater fuel capacity and more powerful engines (the original Pan Am six aircraft were also modified to A standard). Pan Am, however, relinquished three of their ordered Boeings to BOAC in

12 G-AFCX Clyde (above)
13 G-AFCZ Clare (below)
(Ordered by Imperial airways and originally to be named Canterbury.*)* It was agreed that this aircraft would be allocated to the Australian national airline, Qantas, and it was renamed Australia. *Before delivery and re-registration the outbreak of war caused Imperial Airways to retain the aircraft, again renamed* Clare. BOAC, the new Corporation which took over from Imperial Airways, returned to transatlantic operation to America with a further two Short S30s, Clyde *and* Clare, *with long distance fuel tanks and a further increase in maximum take-off weight – now up to 24,040 kilogrammes (53,000 lb). In-flight refuelling would not be used, so that passengers could be carried, limited to three westbound and six eastbound.*

On 3 August 1940 Clare, *commanded by Captain Kelly-Rogers, left Poole Harbour on the first British passenger and mail transatlantic service. The routing was via Foynes, Botwood, Montreal, to La Guardia Airport (marine terminal) in New York. There were several more round trips by the two S30s, the final service being in October, 1940.*

14 Catalina flying boat – *BOAC operated five of this famous type through Foynes. Like the other British based flying boats they helped considerably in shuttling loads for the transatlantic flying boats which terminated at Foynes. The five were: G-AGBJ, G-AGDA, G-AGFL, G-AGFM and G-AGIE. In 1943 the Catalinas were transferred to operate the then longest scheduled run, from Kogala Lake (Perth) to Ceylon.*

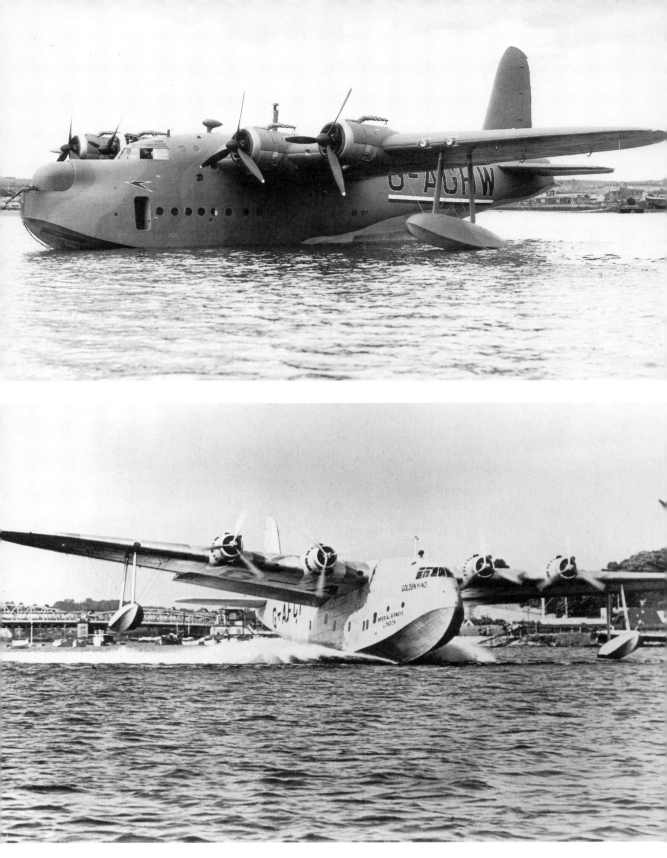

15 Short S25 Sunderland (above)

15 Short S25 Sunderland (above)
– This was the type most often seen
at Foynes and frequently filled the role
of shuttle between Poole Harbour and
Foynes. Fourteen S25s operated
through Foynes during the war years,
and most of them returned to BOAC
afterwards as 'Hythe' aircraft, to be
used on BOAC's eastern routes for
many more years to come.

order to help them with their transatlantic problem. The three transferred were: NC18607, NC18608 and NC18610, to be re-registered and named, respectively, G-AGBZ (*Bristol*), G-AGCA (*Berwick*), G-AGCB (*Bangor*).

Late in 1940 BOAC re-opened their transatlantic route to America, using the modified Short C class S30s, *Clyde* and *Clare*, with increased fuel tankage, but without in-flight refuelling so that a limited number of passengers could be carried.

Starting in 1941 all of BOAC's flying boats based in Britain operated through Foynes, to Lisbon and points beyond, and eventually across the Atlantic to America. The flights originated at the Corporation's flying boat base at Poole Harbour, in Dorset.

First of the wartime fleets of civil flying boats were the Short S30C class Empire boats; then came the twin engined Catalinas, the Short Sunderland S25s, the G class S26s and, of course, the three majestic Boeing 314A flying boats. All were civil aircraft, in wartime camouflage, operated by BOAC crews in BOAC uniform. With the exception of the three Boeing 314As, all were sparsely furnished, the better to support the war effort by maximizing the amount of fuel and payload carried. And, as will be seen, all helped to keep scheduled Atlantic flights going between Britain and America by acting as shuttles between Foynes and Poole for the two American operators who terminated their flights at Foynes.

BOAC, with its fleets of transiting flying boats, was the airline which provided the equipment and handling facilities at Foynes – staff, catering, maintenance, passenger launches and buses, etc. – for itself and for the two American based airlines. Pan Am had returned to an increased schedule to New York in May 1941, using its Boeing 314As – they had nine in all – and American Export Airlines began operations in 1942.

BOAC's Boeings

BOAC's first Boeing 314A, G-AGBZ *Bristol*, was delivered by Captain Kelly-Rogers on 22 May 1941, and the other two aircraft were delivered within a further few months. Pan Am provided aircrew training and the Boeing Flight was based at Baltimore, with Captain Kelly-Rogers as flight manager. BOAC maintained transatlantic service with these aircraft, via Foynes and Botwood, for about seven months of each year, and during the winter months via the southern routes (eastbound via Bermuda, direct to Foynes if upper winds permitted), or via the Azores or Lisbon or both. Westbound winter routing was via Foynes, Lisbon, Bathurst (now Banjul) in Gambia, Belem (Brazil), Trinidad, Bermuda, and on to Baltimore.

16 The S26 Short G class flying
boat (below) – Three S26 aircraft -
well stretched from the C class and
Sunderland family – were built by
Shorts for BOAC, with transatlantic
capability in view. The three were,
G-AFCI (Golden Hind), G-AFCJ
(Golden Fleece) and G-AFCK
(Golden Horn). They were taken
over by the RAF and never saw
Atlantic service. Golden Fleece was
destroyed by early enemy action, and
the remaining two 'G' class, as they
were called, were returned to BOAC.
After a short time with BOAC,
Golden Horn crashed during a test
flight at Lisbon, leaving Golden
Hind the sole fleet survivor.

The coming of Amex

The third airline to be based at Foynes, American Export Airlines (a subsidiary of the shipping company of the similar name, American Export Lines), was ready to start Atlantic services in May 1942, having been licensed to compete with Pan American between New York and Europe, using Foynes as their European base. Amex, as they were

17 BOAC's Boeing 314A,
flagship **Bristol** – *At last BOAC
had a worthy transatlantic challenger.
The 'Boeing boys' were regarded as
the elite of BOAC, even wearing
different – special American-made –
uniforms to 'ordinary' staff. The
standard crew comprised two pilots
(usually both senior captains), two
navigators, two flight engineers, two
radio officers and, 'downstairs', one
purser and two stewards. The purser,
captain of the lower deck, really was a
purser (a trained traffic officer with
responsibility for all documents
including preparation of weight and
balance forms), and not, as some
airlines use the term today, a chief
steward.*

18 The Vought–Sikorsky 44A flying boat – *From Captain Charles Blair's autobiography,* Red Ball in the Sky, *the first American Export Airlines westbound flight from Foynes 22 June 1942, on a VS44A flying boat, is described:*

> We set out from Foynes on this longest of summer days, without any special ambition. The big Sikorsky's fuel tanks were a few hundred gallons short of their 3820-gallon capacity when the sea-plane slipped moorings to ease into the riptide that raced through the narrow west channel between Foynes Island and the south bank of the Shannon. The flight plan called for a fuel stop at Botwood in Newfoundland, on the Bay of Exploits, some 14 hours away.
>
> An onlooker on the shore might have thought that this heavily laden flying boat was more likely to go to the bottom of the broad river than fly safely across the ocean. The hull was so deeply submerged by the full load that the passenger windows were only inches above water level. At the beginning of the take-off a huge wave flared out from the bow to enshroud the ship so heavily with spray that only the wing tips and top of the tail were visible. Finally, seeking release from its briny surroundings, the hull lumbered heavily onto the step at a mile a minute clip and began to skim across the water towards its hundred mile an hour take-off speed. On this cool June evening a brisk west wind streaked the waters of Ireland's fabled river Shannon. I pulled back strenuously on the controls as *Excalibur* climbed quickly into hydroplaning position, then swept majestically down river towards Loop Head and the North Atlantic.

On this flight – which had a number of VIPs on board – both Botwood and Shediac went below safety limits for landing, owing to fog, and the flight made New York non-stop (with only a little fuel left in the tanks).

The man and the aircraft were legends both.

19 Preparing for a shuttle departure, 1943 style — Two stewardesses, wearing BOAC uniform and forage caps, about to board a Sunderland flying boat at Poole Harbour, Peggy Keyte on the left, with Helen Wigmore, plus their catering equipment for the short trip to Foynes, where the passengers would re-embark for the transatlantic flight and the Sunderland would pick up an eastbound transatlantic load for return to Poole.

known in those days, operated three Vought Sikorsky 44A flying boats – the only three ever to be built. With capacity payload they frequently flew New York/Foynes and Bermuda/Foynes non-stop, and even the 'uphill' leg, Foynes/New York against strong headwinds.

Known as the 'Flying Aces', the three Sikorsky aircraft were: NC41880 *Excalibur*; NC41881 *Excambian* and NC41882 *Exeter*. They were the longest range commercial aircraft in the service of any airline and the only aircraft that had flown commercial schedules non-stop with a capacity payload across the North and South Atlantic on flights in excess of 3100 miles (4988 km).

The airline's chief pilot, Charles Blair, had long been associated with the VS44As. As test pilot he had conducted all the flight test work on *Excalibur* for Sikorsky Aircraft, and for the American Civil Aviation Authority certification. He commanded the first American Export flight from New York non-stop to Foynes on 26 May 1942, and flew the VS44As throughout the war years. An outstanding personality, he was, without a doubt, the most popular of all the aircrew who operated through Foynes.

In the winter months American Export took full advantage of the prevailing winds, when eastbound from New York, using what is known as the 'best time-track' to fly non-stop from New York or Bermuda to Foynes (best time-track is using upper winds to advantage to produce the best time; it is not necessarily the shortest distance), avoiding the frozen en route Canadian bases, and using the Azores when necessary. Winter westbound routings, as in the case of BOAC and Pan Am, had to be via a much longer southern route because of frozen landing areas and excessive headwinds on the

Boeing 707 turbo fan—This was an improved model of the 707 Intercontinental that became the longest range jet in commercial service.
The first 707/320C was placed in service in June 1963 by Pan Am.

*Above: Lockheed Tristar in the latest livery
—British Airways operate 15 of this type.*

*Right: Pan American's latest livery on Boeing
747SP (SP=special performance)—For
many years the trend has been to 'stretch'
existing aircraft, but the 747SP reversed this.
The special performance 747 is shorter than
the standard 747 by 14.32m (47 ft), carrying
80 to 100 fewer passengers. It was designed
both for the very long range intercontinental
routes and for those other routes whose traffic
did not require the standard high-capacity
747s. The first of the SPs flew on 4 July
1975 and entered service with Pan Am in
April 1976.*

*Opposite page: Boeing 747/300 (SUD)—
SUD=stretched upper deck. First service of
the 747/300 was in March 1983. The
747/300 features a 7.11m (280 in) structural
extension to the unique upper deck cabin—a
10 per cent increase in seating capacity. The
new upper deck can accommodate up to 69
economy seats, 26 first class or 42 business
class seats.*

The Boeing 767/200— This is the extended-range form (the 200ER), a contender for future transatlantic schedules.

The TWA terminal is an outstanding building sited in the JFK/New York International airport.

northern track. American Export's routing was via Port Lyautey (near Rabat, Morocco), Bathurst (Gambia), Trinidad, and on to New York.

The busy Shannon years

1942 and 1943 saw the greatest activity at Foynes. To quote from Captain Blair's book, *Red Ball in the Sky*, 'The neutral port of Foynes, a sleepy Irish village on the south bank of the River Shannon, ranked in the war years as one of the world's foremost air terminals. Here the flying boats of Pan Am, BOAC and American Export embarked and disembarked the high and low brass of the allied war effort.'

The constant flow of VIPs heightened the feeling among the resident ground staff that they were cut off from the rest of the country – in part, this was true, as motorized transport and telephones were rather scarce! However, there was the bonus of feeling part of the operation of the big flying boats which did not so much come and go but moored and slipped. Those staff lucky enough to own serviceable bicycles were able to use rare days off on visits to neighbouring villages; the energetic ones could even cycle to Limerick city and back in a day, a round trip of 48 miles (77 km). BOAC had problems of communication for with staff billetted around the village – almost all without telephones – it was difficult to advise them of early aircraft arrivals. Signalled flight plans, giving the departure time from the airport of origin and ETA (estimated time of arrival) at Foynes, frequently arrived only minutes before the aircraft. The problem was solved by hiring a local gentleman with his own transport (a horse), whose duty it was to liaise with the operations duty room (which had 24-hour coverage), and when a good estimate of probable arrival time of aircraft was assessed – by whatever means – he would set off on his horse to every residence on his list for that day to spread the glad tidings. With aircraft arriving at first light (night flying being essential because of possible enemy activity), the call during summertime could be as early as 3 am, so the horseman was far from popular. The gentleman also doubled as a baggage loader (without the horse).

It seems unbelievable now that a small area of a neutral country should have been such a hive of wartime activity, carried out in secrecy, for there was never a word of Foynes or Rineanna in the Irish press or radio of the day. Apart from airport workers, only a fairly small section of the population actually witnessed the comings and goings of aircraft, soon taken for granted and scarcely noticed.

The wartime shuttle service

The busiest airline on the Shannon scene was BOAC, committed to provide handling and equipment, not only for their own extensive aircraft movements, but also for the two Foynes based American airlines. The Atlantic traffic was between America and Britain, but both Pan Am and American Export terminated their flights at Foynes, and BOAC's Boeing 314As also often terminated at Foynes. Therefore, for most of the transatlantic flying boats, eastbound loads

**20 The De Havilland DH91
Albatross** – *Flagship of the fleet
known as the 'Frobisher class' by
Imperial Airways and their successor,
BOAC. The Frobishers were elegant
aircraft, built of wood like their
famous military cousins, the
Mosquitoes. Originally intended as a
transatlantic landplane, five of these
aircraft had been inherited by BOAC
from Imperial Airways and by late
1940 three remained: G-AFDJ
(*Falcon*), G-AFDK (*Fortuna*) and
G-AFDM (*Fiona*). All three were
used extensively as shuttles for the
transatlantic flying boats, between
Whitchurch Airport (near Bristol) and
Rineanna, from early 1942. In July
1943, G-AFDK (*Fortuna*)
experienced difficulties while circling
Rineanna before landing in a field
beside a well-known pub (in fact,
Rineanna's local). None of the
passengers or crew were seriously
injured but* Fortuna *was a write-off
and the incident grounded the
remaining two Frobishers for good.*

(passengers, baggage, mail, cargo) were disembarked at Foynes, and westbound loads were embarked there. BOAC's extra responsibility was to provide shuttle aircraft to transport loads from America to a base in the United Kingdom, and loads originating in the United Kingdom for America, to Foynes for embarkation. These flying boats were big load carriers for the time, especially the Boeing 314As which often carried about 6000 kg (13,227 lb), or the equivalent of 65 passengers and their baggage; the shuttle commitment was therefore high, frequently requiring two aircraft for one flying boat service.

Where possible, BOAC used their own flying boats as shuttle aircraft so that both passengers and mail could be disembarked and re-embarked for Britain or America at the same airport.

The peak-time activity at Foynes spilt over into the other part of Shannon Airport, Rineanna, the land plane base across the river, because BOAC, for operational reasons, used many land plane shuttles for the transatlantic flying boats. These BOAC flights originated at Whitchurch Airport, near Bristol, later switched to Croydon (London), and finally operated from Hurn (the land plane base of Bournemouth Airport, of which Poole Harbour was the base for flying boats). The land plane shuttle operation involved the movement of staff, passengers, baggage, mail and cargo by road between the two bases of Shannon Airport, Foynes and Rineanna, a 40-mile (64-km) journey, with baggage, mail and cargo making the trip under customs' seal. At a later date, Aer Lingus undertook much of the traffic handling at Rineanna.

How not to handle VIPs!

Passengers in transit to and from America frequently had long stop-overs at Shannon for operational reasons, weather or mechanical delays. For such long transits it was policy to book the passengers into a local hotel, first choice always being the Dunraven Arms at Adare, a delightful village in County Limerick, about 10 miles (16 km) from Foynes. One such load of passengers, en route from Foynes to Adare, encountered an unscheduled delay when passing through another village on the way. Much to the embarrassment of the BOAC traffic officer accompanying the passengers there was a cattle fair in progress at this village. It took a very long time to get through the narrow village street, crowded with local farmers, each, apparently, with several hundred head of cattle for sale! After that incident, before moving passengers to Adare, there was always a careful check for cattle fairs in progress, with alternative coach routings planned, if necessary.

Westbound problems for the flying boats

The wartime scheduled civil flying boats on the Atlantic – the big Boeing 314As of Pan Am and BOAC, and the long range VS44As of American Export – experienced many problems. With big piston engines there was much that could fail mechanically. Communications were often poor, and terminal and en route weather reports were frequently slow to be transmitted. Besides these factors inducing

ground delays, the one feature which had catastrophic effects on the westbound Atlantic flying was the constant headwind situation caused by the prevailing westerlies.

The effect on these wartime transport aircraft bears little relation to the effect of the same wind force on a typical jet operation of today. The slower an aircraft, the more difficult it becomes to ride the headwinds. This can be seen by comparing three different aircraft types – a wartime flying boat, a subsonic jet (such as a Boeing 707, or any of the wide-bodied aircraft), and a supersonic jet, such as a Concorde, cruising at twice the speed of sound. Sector distance is assumed to be 2000 st (statute) miles (3200 km), which is about the distance between Shannon and Gander, or Foynes and Botwood, and time difference for each type is based on zero wind and a headwind effect of 35 mph (56 kph). In these conditions, the wartime flying boat's time would be increased by well over three hours in a 35 mph headwind, over a zero wind. The subsonic jet would have an increase in time of arrival of about 15 minutes, and the delay for the supersonic jet would be very small – about three or four minutes.

21 The Armstrong Whitworth Ensign – Flagship Ensign – *The* Ensign *was the other ex-Imperial Airways type (in addition to the DH91) to take part in the wartime landplane shuttle programme between Britain and Rineanna. The* Ensign *was a big aircraft – the largest commercial aircraft built in Britain between the wars. The flagship was photographed at Croydon Airport.*

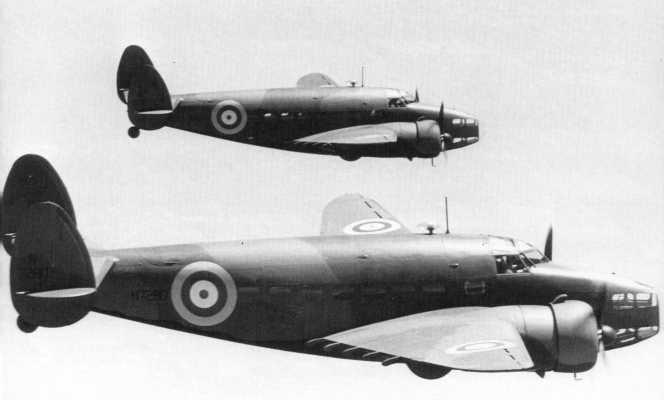

22 Converted Whitley bomber (above) – *The type operated as shuttles for the transatlantic flying boats, Whitchurch/Rineanna/ Whitchurch in early 1943.*

The point of no return

There was a strong tendency for all scheduled westbound flying boats of the three operators to carry the highest possible fuel reserves, and one item in the flight plan was kept under constant review – the PNR (point of no return). Up to this point, based on forecast upper winds, the aircraft could return to its point of departure with required planned fuel reserves, but once past the point the crew would have to proceed to their destination or decide to return to the departure airport with less reserves than planned. The greater the reserves of fuel, the further the aircraft could go before the crew decided to return to the departure airport, and, of course, the better would be the chance of their coping with unexpected headwinds.

Aircraft returning to departure point was not exactly an unusual occurrence at that time, and a call-out arrangement for ground staff to cover the contingency was in force at Foynes (invariably the same people who had been on duty for the departure). On one such occasion an aircraft, Botwood-bound from Foynes, was forced to return to Foynes. It arrived back some 12 hours after its departure and was met by the same BOAC traffic officer who had seen the departure off. One of the passengers, on disembarking, stared at the BOAC traffic officer and exclaimed, 'Good heavens – there's a chap exactly like you who saw us off from Foynes!' The lucky gentleman had slept for most of the 12 hours and never heard the cabin crew announcement about returning to Foynes.

Gander and the Return Ferry Service

Gander International Airport, Newfoundland, has experienced many changes of name, first being known as 'the airport at Hattie's Camp near Gander Lake'! When construction began in 1936 it was named Newfoundland Airport; in 1940, after the arrival of the RCAF, the airport became Gander Airport. The new town, constructed west of the airport, took the name Gander.

On 1 April 1941, Newfoundland handed over control of Gander Airport to Canada for the duration of the war. The airport fulfilled its original role as a transatlantic air terminal in serving as a base for the ferry operations during the war years. With Gander as the key airport, the transatlantic ferry service proved a great success, with more than 16,000 aircraft safely delivered to Britain by the RAF and the USAF.

In the early war days, the regular Atlantic ferry crews were returned from Britain by boat (the ferrying being strictly one-way). This took up to 14 days and created an unacceptable back-log of deliveries. Plans were made to fly the crews back from Britain, heralding the creation of the Return Ferry Service. The most suitable military aircraft for the job was the American built Consolidated B24, known as the *Liberator*. Seven of these aircraft were put into service, operated by BOAC – sometimes flown with mixed RAF and BOAC crews – constituting the first all-year-round North Atlantic passenger and freight service. This was a big improvement in continuity over the flying boat service which, as we have seen, had to fly during winter

23 Lockheed Hudsons with RAF markings (below) – *Hudsons operated with BOAC and flew on the wartime shuttle route Whitchurch/ Rineanna/Whitchurch and, later, using Croydon as a British terminal.*

24 Dakota/DC3 – Eventually
BOAC operated just one type of
landplane shuttle on the wartime
Britain/Rineanna shuttle service, the
ubiquitous Douglas DC3 (the
wartime Dakota), from the British
bases of Whitchurch and Croydon to
Rineanna, in tandem with the flying
boat shuttle service between Foynes
and Poole Harbour (Bournemouth).
Towards the end of wartime flying,
the BOAC Dakotas shuttled between
Hurn (the landplane part of
Bournemouth Airport) and Rineanna.
This Dakota is in post-war BEA
livery.

25 Aerial view of Gander Airport –
At the time it was constructed,
Gander was the largest airport site in
the world, being one mile square. In
the summer of 1940 Gander became
the main staging post for the delivery
of aircraft to Britain. By mid-1943
Gander was:

> much the largest RCAF
> operational base in history, with
> a population occasionally
> reaching past 15,000, counting
> RCAF, USAF, RAF,
> Canadian army, contractors and
> local civilian personnel
> employed.

(Air Marshal Annis, Commanding
Officer, Gander, 1955).
Gander was 'demilitarized' at the end
of the Second World War, and by the
end of 1946 it was estimated that
1,000 passengers a day passed through
the airport.

47

26 A B24 Consolidated Liberator converted bomber at Prestwick Airport – The Liberator was used by BOAC for the wartime Return Ferry Service between Prestwick in Ayrshire and Dorval, Montreal, with intermediate stops as and when necessary at Keflavik, Iceland, Gander, Newfoundland and Goose Bay, Labrador.

27 Boeing 307 Stratoliner – The final 307 configuration only differed from early B17s (Flying Fortresses) in fuselage design. The 307 was the first aircraft to use cabin pressurization for passenger comfort (normal atmospheric pressure was maintained at high altitude). TWA operated five of these aircraft, designated S-307Bs, which were drafted into the United States Army Air Transport Command as C75s and flown world-wide by TWA crews. Their three years of service included 3000 Atlantic crossings. The C75s were returned to the Boeing factory in 1944 for conversion to airline standards and, after extensive modifications, were re-designated SA-307B-1s. They remained in TWA service until 1951.

28 *TWA stewardesses in the late*
1930s.

**29 TWA cabin crew in the late
1970s** — The airline introduced these

uniforms for its male and female flight
attendants. They are pictured next to

a Lockheed 1011 aircraft.

months via more southerly airports, owing to frozen en route North Atlantic bases.

Gander Airport was – and still is – often shut down rapidly owing to fog reducing visibility below acceptable limits – the fog comes from the nearby Gulf Stream and is difficult to forecast. Another big airport, therefore, was urgently needed, about 300 miles (480 km) north of Gander, close enough to the great circle (shortest possible distance) from the United Kingdom bases to Montreal and New York, and also close to the great circle track from Keflavik, in Iceland, to Montreal and New York. The ideal site was discovered in July 1941, in the wilds of Labrador.

The creation of Goose Bay Airport, Labrador

Goose Bay was built in 1941–42 by the Canadian Government, the site being a sandy plateau 20 miles (32 km) south of North West River. It was a vast undertaking, carried out in the wilds with precision and speed.

The initial headquarters was established at the nearest fur-trading settlement at North West River – an isolated cluster of white wooden buildings grouped around a Hudson Bay Company store, the church and hospital of the Grenfell Mission. The ice-breaker *MacLean* was the first ship to arrive at Goose Bay on 19 August 1941, carrying equipment and staff, followed a month later by three other ships, with bulldozers, prefabricated houses and graders, amongst other things. By November 1941 three gravel runways were available to a length of 2134 m (7000 ft), suitable for large aircraft. Construction continued throughout the winter of 1941–42. Accommodation buildings and hangars were ready by early 1942, and Goose Bay began to play its planned operational role.

Farewell to the scheduled transatlantic flying boats

Towards the end of 1945 the scheduled transatlantic flying boat was phased out. On 22 October, American Export's NC41881 *Excambian* departed from Foynes for New York, on the airline's last scheduled flying boat flight, commanded by Captain Blair who, three years and four months previously, had commanded the first American Export westbound flight from Foynes on NC41880 *Excalibur*. American Export's next transatlantic scheduled flight was a DC4 landplane, through Rineanna two days later – almost an overnight changeover!

Pan Am's last flying boat schedule from Foynes was their Boeing 314A, NC18609, on 29 October 1945. The day before the departure of NC18609, on 28 October, marked Pan Am's first scheduled landplane flight on the *Atlantic*, a DC4 which transited Rineanna. All future Pan Am services were to be operated by landplane across the North Atlantic. The 314A flying boats were eventually sold to American based companies.

BOAC kept their three Boeing 314As operating on the southern route a little longer, before transferring them to the Baltimore/Bermuda Service. The famous trio, *Bristol*, *Berwick* and *Bangor* were sold in 1948, having completed 596 Atlantic crossings and carried 42,000 passengers without accident or injury.

Of American Export's trio of Flying Aces, the flagship *Excalibur* was lost at Botwood in 1943, leaving her two sister ships to fulfil Atlantic schedules for the remainder of the war. *Exeter*, while allegedly involved in gun-running in the hands of new owners, was lost in Uruguay in 1947. The sole survivor of the fleet, *Excambian* was leased to Captain Blair in 1947. In addition to being a scheduled airline captain he was, at that time, also running a charter airline, and used the aircraft to fly personnel and equipment to Keflavik Airport, in Iceland, where the air base was still being developed. Having been passed on to another owner after the Iceland contract, *Excambian* was again acquired by Captain Blair in January 1968, this time for his Caribbean based airline, Antilles Air Boats, in the Virgin Islands. In 1976 the aircraft was donated by Captain Blair to the Naval Air Museum in Pensacola, Florida. *Excambian* is now in the process of being lovingly restored to her former glory by United Technologies/Sikorsky Aircraft, of Stratford, Connecticut, and will soon be on view at the New England Air Museum at Windsor Locks, Connecticut.

In 1945 Atlantic scheduled flights became the province of the land-plane. Year-round operation between Europe and North America

30 Dorval Airport (Montreal International Airport) – In December 1940, it was decided to develop an airport at Dorval as a civil air terminal for the metropolitan area of Montreal, the cost of the work to be borne jointly by the Department of Transport and the Department of National Defence. The first contract for the job was awarded on 10 October 1940. Dorval Airport opened on 1 September 1941, with three runways completed. A fast job by any standards!

31 Peak period during the war years at Prestwick Airport (above) – Prestwick was very much part of the North Atlantic conquest during the war – both westbound and eastbound and in all seasons, being the European terminal for BOAC's Return Ferry Service. The airport was established as the British terminal for the wartime Atlantic Ferry Service because of its strategic location and its good weather record. Prestwick also became an important staging point on the pioneering post-war North Atlantic scheduled services, the main users being BOAC, TCA, KLM and SAS (the Scandinavian flag carrier).

had become a practical proposition, thanks to the vast wartime experience of a great number of aviators, both civil and service, the constant improvement of aircraft and aeroplane engines, and the airports which had appeared in the right places at the right time.

32 Avro Lancastrian (below) – TCA (now Air Canada) used Lancastrians (converted Lancaster bombers) as Atlantic mail carriers during the war years, laying the foundation for their post-war North Star scheduled services.

Chapter 1 1945–1950:

The landplane schedules take shape

33 Douglas DC4 – this was the aircraft which permitted the rapid transition from flying boat to landplane on the North Atlantic routes. Known as the 'Skymaster', most of the immediate post-war aircraft in airline service were de-militarized Air Force C54s. The DC4 epitomized the success story of the 'family' type development, stretching through the various models to come of the DC6 and DC7.

The world's first duty free shop

With the closure of Foynes flying boat base, the name of Rineanna also disappeared, and Shannon Airport now referred solely to the landplane base in County Clare. Appointed by the Irish Government, Mr Brendan O'Regan, who had already made his mark on Foynes in the build-up of passenger facilities, went on to guide the formation of the Shannon Free Airport Development Company, leading to the establishment of the first Customs Free Airport in 1947 and the international shopping centre, the world's first duty free shop. Shannon had acquired a very special image with transatlantic travellers, thanks to Brendan O'Regan's drive and initiative. Later on, the sales and catering organization became the responsibility of Aer Rianta (Irish Airports).

**34 and 35 Transatlantic plus –
TWA DC4** (right) – This plane
inaugurated commercial service
between America and Egypt, 1 April
1946, from Washington, DC via
New York, Gander, Shannon, Paris,
Rome and Athens. From the military
C69 came the first of the Lockheed
Constellations, the model 049
(below). TWA's inaugural Atlantic
flight on 5 February 1946 from La
Guardia Airport, New York, to
Paris, was routed via Gander and
Shannon. The pressurized
Constellation, with its streamlined
aerodynamic design and four powerful
Wright engines, was the most
advanced aircraft of its day.

36 BOAC's Constellations –
Starting in July 1946, BOAC at last
filled the gap for flights from Britain to
America and back, by restarting their
scheduled flights, using Lockheed 049
Constellations. The fleet was based at
Dorval Airport, Montreal, and

initially consisted of five aircraft:
G-AHEJ, G-AHEK, G-AHEL,
G-AHEM and G-AHEN. A short
time later, a sixth 049 was added to
the fleet, G-AKCE. The
Constellations were scheduled to
Canada, as well as America, from

Britain, and later to Bermuda and the
Caribbean.

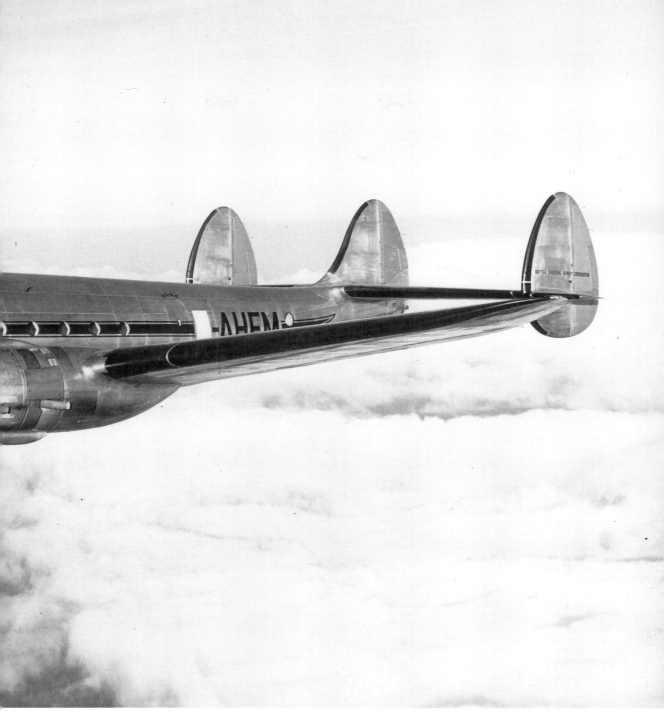

A new sort of passenger and new airlines

Travel-starved tourists from both sides of the Atlantic were eager to make use of the post-war transatlantic schedules; the operators were not short of payload, nor were they likely to be for many years, with sharp increases in the number of passengers expected. Of the three wartime scheduled operators, BOAC continued to operate the

37 The North Star – *The Canadair North Star was a familiar sight on the North Atlantic routes in the 1940s and 1950s, operated by Trans Canada Airlines (TCA). The North Star was basically a DC4, modified and using Rolls-Royce Merlin engines. The aircraft were also known as Canadairs, and later models were pressurized. BOAC used the type extensively (they were known as Argonauts), but not on Atlantic schedules.*

38 BOAC Liberator – *Here the Liberator appears at Dorval Airport Montreal, in a snow storm, in 1945.*

Liberators between Prestwick and Montreal, while Pan Am and American Export continued their America/Europe link via Gander and Shannon to Hurn Airport (Bournemouth) in Britain. These two airlines were soon joined on the Atlantic route by a third American operator, TWA (then the abbreviation for Transcontinental and Western Air, from 1950 it meant Trans-World Airlines – a more apt title). TWA operated from New York via Gander and Shannon to Paris, Rome, and on to many other airports, as far east as Bombay.

By the end of 1945 the name 'American Export' disappeared from the aviation scene, as the airline was acquired by one of the powerful American domestic carriers, American Airlines, and the new transatlantic airline became American Overseas Airlines (shortened to AOA), routing from Washington, DC and Chicago to Hurn Airport in Britain.

Competition increases for the American carriers

Significant developments on the Atlantic scene were now not far away – the opening to international traffic of London's Heathrow Airport, and increased competition from European based operators for the three established American based operators.

BOAC, with their new fleet of Constellations scheduled to America and Canada, presented strong competition, and further competition came from Air France. By June 1946 a new European operator had also appeared on the scene, SABENA, the Belgian flag carrier. Later in the year, TCA (now Air Canada) began scheduled operations through to Shannon, to complement their already established Prestwick operation, using North Star aircraft. KLM (the Royal Dutch airline) and Swissair were soon to join the transatlantic

39 TWA Constellation – The Constellation is flying past the pyramids of Gizeh, on the Chicago to Cairo service in 1946.

operators using Shannon, now very much the hub of transatlantic flying, and referred to as 'Europe's aircraft carrier'.

By July 1950, ten international scheduled carriers operated through Shannon on the North Atlantic route: Pan American, American Overseas, TWA, BOAC, Air France, SABENA, TCA, Swissair, KLM and LAI (the Italian flag carrier). A short time later, the name American Overseas Airlines disappeared from the Atlantic routes, its personnel, routes and aircraft taken over by Pan American.

The building of Heathrow

The aviation history of the area known as Heathrow, now one of the world's busiest airports, really began in 1929, when Richard Fairey's Great West Aerodrome was developed and used mainly for experimental flying. In 1942 a survey of possible sites was begun for a large airfield for wartime needs near London, and the area north east of Stanwell was chosen.

In 1944 Heathrow was conceived when work began on a military airfield based on a triangular pattern of runways. The war ended before the airfield could be put to military use, and it became necessary to replan for civil purposes.

A committee of experts was appointed to decide the airport's development. It will be appreciated how difficult it was to assess

40 Heathrow – This is a very early Heathrow scene. Airport facilities were housed in tents and caravans.

future civil aviation requirements after six years of war, with the great unknowns of the future influence of the jet engine and whether flying boats would have a place in the scheme of things to come (many thought they would).

Different runway combinations were considered for integration with the existing triangular system at Heathrow, and two factors had to be considered carefully: firstly, the runway pattern had to minimize crosswind for take-off and landing; and secondly, the runway pattern had, desirably, to be duplicated, utilizing parallel runways to permit simultaneous take-offs and landings. The result was the runway pattern, the double triangle, known as the Star of David, a plan which was abandoned in 1952.

On 1 January 1946 a British South American Airways Lancastrian took off from Heathrow with Buenos Aires as the ultimate destination. The commander was Captain D.C.T. Bennett, who also flew the first payload across the Atlantic and commanded the first Liberator of the BOAC Return Ferry Service. It is argued, however, that the airport had not been officially opened then, and the BSAA trip was a proving flight, so that the honour should go to BOAC for the first scheduled flight in May 1946.

Since the formal opening, constant planning, on a bewildering scale, has become necessary to keep pace with the growth of air traffic, with constructional development constantly under way. It is incredible that the airport has been kept continually operational, in spite of the ever changing trends in aircraft design and travel pattern.

All three runways in the original triangle were operational by 1947. Work continued on the second triangle, phased with the construction of a tunnel under the number one runway. The early terminal buildings on the north side (on the Bath Road) were of temporary construction so that they could later be replaced. A plan for a permanent terminal complex was prepared and Heathrow Airport, as we now know it, began to take shape in 1950.

41 Boeing Stratocruiser model 377 – *This was the airliner counterpart of the C97 and the first commercial Boeing aircraft produced since the 314 flying boat. Fifty-six Stratocruisers were built at Boeing's Seattle plant, 1947–49, side by side with B50 bombers, using powerplants and systems similar to those of the B50 and adaptions of the proven C97 airframe. The Stratocruiser offered long range and unparalleled passenger comfort, a lower-deck lounge reached by a spiral stairway from the passenger cabin, a complete galley for hot meal service, a pressurized cabin permitting comfortable flying conditions at up to 7620 metres (25,000 ft) and an enormous forward hold, accessible in flight. The maximum allowable take-off weight was, for the day, a fantastic 66,134 kg (145,800 lb).*

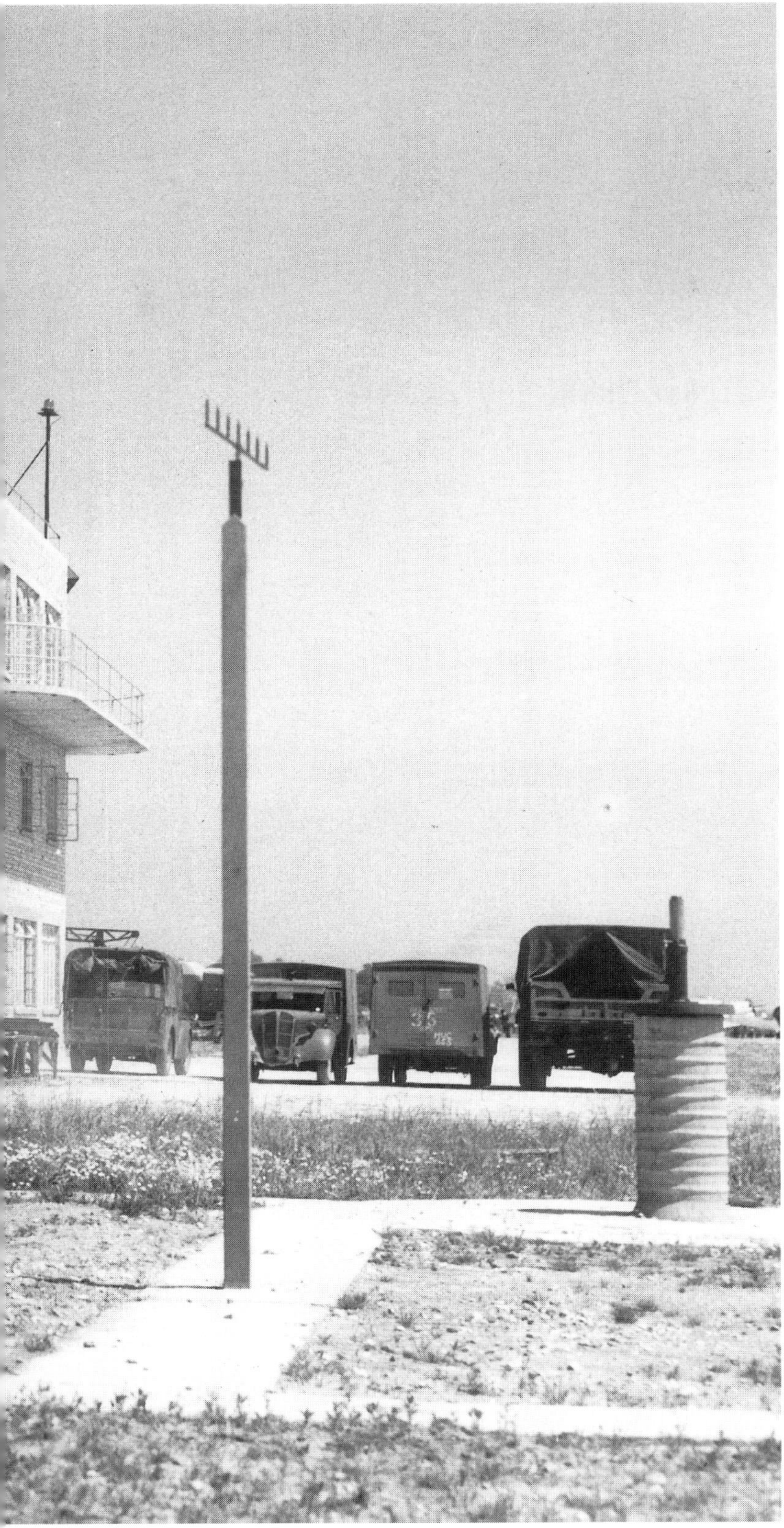

42 Control tower, Heathrow – *In the very early days.*

TWA INTERNATIONAL ROUTES 1946

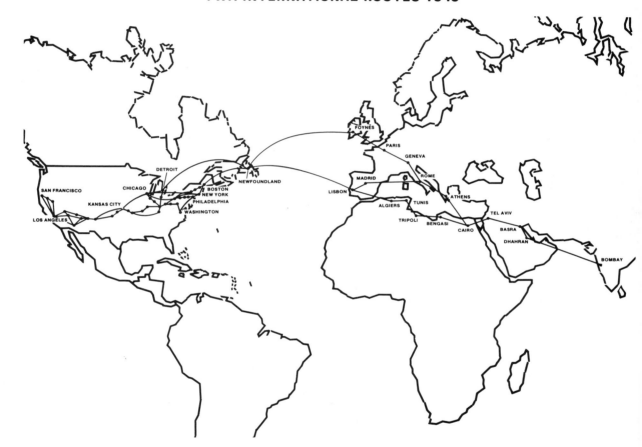

43 Control tower, Heathrow (top) – *well into the wide-body era.*
TWA Route Map *(1946) shows*

what a trail-blazing airline can achieve, once the Atlantic ocean segment is mastered. Within a year of its first international flight, TWA was providing passenger service across the Azores, Bombay, Cairo, Dhahran

(Persian Gulf), Geneva, Lisbon,

Madrid, Paris, Rome, Shannon, Tel Aviv, Tripoli and Tunis, flying Lockheed Constellation and Douglas DC4 aircraft. Interestingly, Shannon Airport is marked as 'Foynes'; although the marine base was then closed, the internationally known name lingered on.

Chapter 2 up to 1952:

Opening of New York International and Atlantic routing problems

Idlewild gets under way

> The greatest airport in the world is rising from the meadows at Idlewild in New York City. It will cost $71 million. Filling, grading, planting, drainage, field lighting utilities, runways, taxiways and aprons, will cost about $35 million. The administrative building, together with loading docks, apron and parking spaces will cover well over 300 acres and cost about $10 million.
>
> The airport will bring millions of dollars monthly in commerce, business and traffic to the city of New York. When in full operation thirty thousand passengers will go through its gates daily. Many tons of mail, express and freight will be handled. Forty thousand men and women will be permanently employed in airport activities. The airport is a costly undertaking, yet it will be one of the best investments the city ever made. It will pay its way.

These words were spoken by Mayor Fiorello La Guardia of New York in early 1945 at the time concrete was being poured for the main runway at Idlewild Airport. The Idlewild site was 14 miles (22 km) from Times Square, on the west side of Jamaica Bay, directly across from the airfield known as Floyd Bennett Field.

Mayor La Guardia had been a champion of aviation for many years, having made possible the airport which bore his name – La Guardia Airport at North Beach, at that time one of the world's busiest airports, but considered unlikely to cope with the expected rush by the travelling public to board commercial airliners in record numbers. This time La Guardia was determined to develop an airport to outlast the twentieth century – ten times bigger than La Guardia Airport, needing 5000 acres (about 20 square km). Sadly, Mayor La Guardia died in 1947, a year before the great new airport opened.

During 1945 Mayor La Guardia was replaced as mayor of New York by William O'Dwyer – not nearly so preoccupied with air transport as his predecessor – and consequently there was a question mark against the future of Idlewild. Many plans were advanced and examined until, in 1946, the planners concurred with Mayor La Guardia that the city needed a new international airport. The Port of New York Authority made a study of both La Guardia and Idlewild Airports, to consider taking over the development and operation of both. On 1 June 1947 the Port Authority signed a 50 year lease with

the city for financing, developing and operating both New York International (Idlewild) and La Guardia Airports, on a self-supporting basis.

Idlewild was dedicated on 31 July 1948, the opening day of a nine-day international air exposition. President Truman, accompanied by many well-known dignitaries, opened the exposition and officially dedicated the airport before an estimated crowd of over 200,000.

The very first passenger aircraft departure from Idlewild was,

44 A Pan Am Constellation
(above) – *Here it flies over New York International/Idlewild terminal building in 1947.*

appropriately, a scheduled flight on the prestige North Atlantic route – an Air France Constellation, bound for Paris.

Keflavik – a key airport

Newer piston engined aircraft such as the Douglas DC6 and the Boeing Stratocruiser, carried more passengers further, but not so much further to avoid technical refuelling stops – especially when westbound – at Prestwick, Shannon, Gander, Goose Bay, and Keflavik in Iceland, a most important en route airport.

Originally known as Meeks Field, Keflavik Airport was constructed by the Americans on a volcanic plain about 35 miles (about 56 km) from the Icelandic capital, Reykjavik. All civil facilities, including the airport hotel, were in one large building. It was agreed that the United States Government would operate the airport and construct roads and buildings to the Icelandic Government's specification. During 1949–50 Lockheed Aircraft Overseas Corporation (LAOC) provided airport ground handling for transiting civil aircraft, but America's Military Air Transport Service (MATS) had overall control, including accommodation, from Washington, DC. Later, Lockheeds left the island, and handling facilities were taken over by the Civil Aviation Administration of Iceland (CAA), while airlines who were regular visitors, such as BOAC, TCA and Pan Am, maintained small, mainly supervisory, maintenance and flight dispatch staff.

Surface wind in the Icelandic summer is about 20 mph (32 kph), and in the winter 35 to 45 mph (56 to 72 kph), with gusts 75 to 90 mph (120 to 144 kph). What is referred to as 'horizontal snow' is frequent in the winter, and the airport ramp would often have made an ideal practice ground for Olympic skaters.

Keflavik provided very good alternative routing, especially for airlines whose destinations were in Canada, as the upper winds to Canada usually permitted an operation without a further stop at Goose Bay or Gander. As many of BOAC's flights were scheduled to Montreal, BOAC used Keflavik extensively. Some BOAC American bound flights transiting Keflavik had to make a further refuelling stop at Gander or Goose Bay, the payloads carried being consistently higher than other transatlantic carriers of the time.

Routine routing problems

Aircraft of the day, when westbound, even though pressurized to fly at 20,000 ft (6096 metres) or higher, were often forced to fly at 10,000 ft (3048 metres), usually because of the much stronger headwinds at higher levels. Frequently it was also necessary to fly the aircraft at an economical speed, slower than the standard speed for cruise using less fuel, in order to accommodate booked payload over the critical sector. (Payload is the term used to describe the weight of the passengers and their baggage, mail and freight.) This cruise procedure was known as LRC (Long Range Cruise). Passengers often had to accept a bumpy ride, as well as a slow one! Atlantic westbound routings depended on payload to be carried, en route and terminal weather conditions and,

45 New York International
(below) – *Another airport finds a use for tents – a mile and a half of them! Left over from the nine day international exposition, the tents were pressed into service soon after the opening of New York International/Idlewild, as temporary air cargo shelters. Originally the tents housed hundreds of exhibits covering every aspect of aviation history, from a model of the Wright Brothers' plane to the latest in radar and jet engines.*

46 President Eisenhower – the
president greets two TWA hostesses
after a flight aboard a Lockheed
Constellation in the early 1950s.

47 SAS DC6B – *The DC6B was pressurized to allow cruising heights up to 7620 metres (25,000 ft), stretched to 3.88 metres (12 ft 9 in.) longer than the DC4, and up to 80 mph (125 kph) faster than that aircraft.*

48 Goose Bay Airport – *Goose Bay projected a feeling of utter isolation on a grand scale. The miracle of the airport construction itself, the harsh arctic winters, the activity in the local village getting huskies and sledges ready for the big freeze each fall – all contributed to the feeling of remoteness. An airport of great character, Goose was a major link in the development of Atlantic flying. After the war, following the signing of a 20-year lease between America and Canada, America undertook an extensive construction programme on the south side of the airport, including hangars, a chapel, a theatre, the 'Goose Hilton' Hotel and a new hospital. (The aircraft lined up are North American F86 Sabre fighters, in transit, en masse.)*

especially (as with the wartime flying boats), the upper wind forecast for the flight plan.

Assuming a flight starting in London with New York as the destination, the main choice of routings would embrace: London/Gander/New York; London/Shannon/Gander/New York; London/Keflavik/New York; London/Keflavik/Goose Bay/New York. Prestwick would often be an alternative to Shannon, but Shannon had the advantage of being closer to Gander. Strange routings sometimes appeared, such as London/Santa Maria (Azores)/Gander/New York, probably indicating that Shannon/Gander was not accessible owing to strong headwinds, and that the Keflavik weather was below company limits. Overall, one westbound refuelling stop appeared inevitable, and two were not unusual. Passengers were briefed that the technical stops were due to 'excessive headwinds', but it was never explained that the 'excessive headwinds' were there nearly all the time. Perhaps the most surprised passengers to end up in an icy Keflavik, as first stop, were those whose final destination was sunny Nassau or Montego Bay, for often, with the aircraft available, the only way to get them there was via Keflavik, Gander (or Goose Bay) and Bermuda.

Chapter 3 1952–1956:

The all tourist aircraft to the non-stopper

49 Tourist DC6B – Interior view of the all tourist DC6B, showing the five abreast seating arrangement.

Pressure from Pan Am for an all tourist aircraft and fare

As far back as 1948, Pan Am started to press for an Atlantic tourist fare and high density seating. The International Air Transport Association (IATA) was looking for unanimous agreement from member states' governments for a tourist service at reduced fares, but the carriers were ill-prepared to start such a service in 1952 – all, that is, except Pan Am. Pan Am's director, Juan Trippe had ordered 18 Douglas DC6Bs in September 1950. The DC6B had stretched fuselage and better take-off weight; it was also faster than its predecessor and had a special passenger configuration – more rows of seats and five abreast seating, thus increasing the passenger accommodation from the usual 52 to 82.

After a great deal of lobbying the new tourist service was agreed on

50 The Douglas DC6B – *A high density seating version of this type, operated by Pan American, made history in 1952, being the first all tourist aircraft to fly Atlantic routes.*

**51 A BOAC Lockheed 049
Constellation** – *The entire fleet of
six aircraft was converted to all tourist
configuration for Atlantic routes.*

with some reluctance, in 1952. BOAC decided to use all their six
Lockheed 049 Constellations for tourist aircraft on the Atlantic
schedules, and had the interiors re-configured by Lockheeds, also
using five abreast seating, boosting the passenger capacity from 43 to
68. The first all tourist service on the Atlantic was a Pan Am DC6B on
1 May 1952. Pan Am called these new schedules the 'Rainbow
Service'.

Early problems of the high density aircraft

The overall effect of the high density tourist aircraft was to increase,
rather than decrease, the number of technical refuelling stops, owing
to the greater payload of passengers. Also, there was less space for fuel
or for the carriage of mail (which had to go). Often excess loads, such
as mail, went on first class aircraft (since there was no space on the
scheduled tourist class), thus reducing the chances of the first class
flight of a one stop westerly crossing. These were the days of very high
load factors (ratio of passengers to seats available). The dreaded

...*AC tourist class* (above) – ...view of BOAC Lockheed 049 ...lation in all tourist lay-out.

53 Heathrow 1953 (below) – *A rapidly developing London Airport/Heathrow in early 1953, with GCA (Ground Controlled Approach, a landing aid utilizing radar, to talk down aircraft in poor weather conditions) equipment in the foreground. In the background is a* BOAC Stratocruiser; BOAC operated ten of this type (including four originally intended for SAS) in a 60-seat, all first class configuration, plus a lounge 'downstairs', with a bar and 12 plush seats. BOAC used their Stratocruisers for a longer period than any other operator of the type.

54 Prestwick Airport (facing page, above) – *Post-war commercial rival to Shannon. However, the two airports were technical partners, forming Shanwick, the main Atlantic control centre for all traffic between Europe and longitude 30 West. (From 30 West westbound, Gander became the controlling agent.)*

55 Lockheed Super Constellation model 1049 in BOAC livery (facing page, below) – *BOAC did not operate the popular stretched Constellation; this particular aircraft had been 'wet leased' (that is, hired complete with crews to fly it and maintenance back-up) from an American carrier, owing to BOAC's temporary shortage of capacity in the mid-1950s, for the New York/Bermuda run.*

56 Lockheed Super Constellation 1049G (this page, above) – *The 'Super G' had a massive stretch of 5.59 metres (18 ft 4 in.) and many other design changes, including more powerful engines and wingtip tanks for greater fuel capacity.*

situation, which hit more than one airline, was to have an aircraft grounded, owing to mechanical problems, at an intermediate technical-stop airport, such as Shannon, Keflavik or Gander, with a full load of passengers and, during the subsequent delay period, other aircraft of the same airline, for the same destination and also fully loaded, transiting the same intermediate airport – as a result there would be no chance of transferring the unfortunate delayed passengers to the operational aircraft. The situation would, of course, be at its worst if the delayed aircraft were all first class, and the parade of transiting aircraft during the delay period were all tourist class! Roll on the 'non-stoppers' – their time had almost come.

The advent of the Douglas DC7C

The expression 'non-stopper' implied that a specific aircraft type was capable of a year-round transatlantic schedule, carrying a full load of passengers, without the necessity of a technical stop for refuelling. In 1956 the Douglas DC7C produced this non-stop aircraft capability, flying from a number of European airports to the airports of the eastern seaboard of America, and to Canadian destinations such as Montreal, Toronto and Ottawa.

Best time-track flight plan concept

Track, in this context, refers to the projection on the earth's surface of the path of an aircraft, which is usually expressed as latitude and

57 The DC7C – *This aircraft with excellent airfield performance and a take-off maximum weight as high as 64,864 kg (143,000 lb), was the first aircraft with Europe/America non-stop capability all year round, and was the final stretch in the Douglas DC piston engined family.*

58 Starliner – *The biggest stretch of the Lockheed Constellation, the L1649 Starliner, came later than the DC7C and also offered non-stop year round transatlantic capability.*

59 Britannia – *The Bristol*
Britannia *turbo-propeller, model 312,*
arrived much too late for the Atlantic
scene. Though faster, quieter, and
with a higher cruising level than the
'non-stopper' piston engined aircraft,
the Britannia *was destined to have a*
brief life as a scheduled Atlantic
aircraft, before being forced to give
way to the jets. A fine aircraft, and
very popular with passengers, the
Britannia *continued on the North*
Atlantic routes for many years as a
charter aircraft.

61 *Aerial view of Dorval Airport, Montreal, in the 1950s.*

longitude over an ocean segment. Following the example of the pilots of the wartime American Export flying boats, flight planners were interested in the fastest possible time from airport to airport, not necessarily the shortest distance, so that forecast upper winds dictated the track to be flown. With the extra flyable distance owing to non-stop capability, use of the best time-track flight plan assumed new importance. Carriers submitted Atlantic flight plans to air traffic control showing the requested latitudes at every ten degrees of longitude. A further refinement of the Atlantic oceanic plan was that latitude would be to the nearest whole latitude, that is, 52.15 degrees North and 52.45 degrees North would have to be 52 North and 53 North, respectively.

Flight plans, dependent on the route chosen would (for example, in the case of London/New York) initially be cleared on an airway (airways are corridors of the air, defined as 'a control area or portion thereof established in the form of a corridor equipped with radio navigation aids'), routed to the correct 'exit' (for example, overhead Shannon), and then would check every ten degrees of longitude on its chosen track, until reaching check point for 'entry' route (for example, overhead Gander), and then the final part of the trip would again be on airways, to New York. The great circle (shortest possible) distance between London and New York is 3440 st miles (5536 km), but the shortest possible distance by air on a properly filed oceanic flight plan, allowing for airways flying, departure and arrival positioning, and the need to check the nearest whole latitude at every ten degrees of longitude during the ocean segment, comes to around 3640 st miles (5860 km).

Once again, a decision by Juan Trippe of Pan American had a powerful impact on the course of Atlantic scheduled flights – the decision to go from piston engined aircraft straight to jets, omitting the apparently logical step of using turbo-propeller aircraft.

Chapter 4 1956–1969:

The coming of the jets

'Stretched runways' needed for stretched aircraft

In October 1955 Pan American ensured that the world should enter the jet age, by placing orders for 25 Douglas DC8s and 23 Boeing 707s (thus neatly sewing up both production lines for some time to come). The international competition had no choice but to follow their leader. The new jet breed would fly twice as high as the displaced piston engined aircraft, almost twice as fast with double the payload, and with capacious cargo holds to carry vastly more cargo and mail in addition to the normal passenger baggage. The revolution was under way, another clear 'first' for Pan American who had staked their lot on the success of the big jets.

For a short time there was a return to refuelling stops at Shannon, Keflavik and Gander, as the early jet aircraft did not have sufficient range to be sure of flying from America to Europe and back in one go. The words 'runway limited' were often heard, indicating that a runway was not long enough for the new jets to become airborne at maximum allowable take-off weight, or at a take-off weight that took into account the extra fuel needed for the longer journey. Airport authorities were therefore starting to think about lengthening existing runways and building new ones. In the meantime the only way to get airborne with a larger load was to create extra thrust by making what was known as a wet take-off. On a dry take-off (without water injection) the engines could only create more thrust than was allowed by the maintenance manual for a very brief period, before overheating. Water injection was therefore used to cool the engines supplying this extra thrust during the critical take-off period.

Unfortunately, 'wet' take-offs created a trail of smoke from the four engines with the aircraft still on the runway. A story was rife that on one occasion four 'wet' take-offs in quick succession from New York International reduced visibility so much (it was already a murky day) that the airport went below landing limits, causing subsequent arrivals, for quite a time, to be diverted to Boston!

Growth of the Boeing and Douglas jet families

In early 1956 Pan Am ordered the Boeing Intercontinental 707/320, and a little later BOAC ordered the Intercontinental 707/420, similar to the 707/320 but with Rolls-Royce Conway engines instead of the 320's Pratt & Whitney engines. The Intercontinental was to be a big

62 De Havilland Comet 4 – This was an update of a mid-40s design. Though the first jet aircraft to operate on the North Atlantic commercially (by a short head), the Comet 4 was never serious competition for either the Douglas DC8 or the Boeing 707, being slower and having less range than the American jets. More importantly, the American aircraft were at the start of their development period. The BOAC Comet 4s flew the North Atlantic schedules for two years, (1958–60) until they were replaced by the Boeing 707/420 series.

63 367–80 (Boeing 707 prototype) – *Known as 'Dash Eighty', this was a mighty milestone in aviation. The prototype carried the designation 367-80 as many of the earlier design studies had evolved from the C97 (model 367, or Stratocruiser, being the civil derivative). The prototype was very much closer to the B47 jet bomber than to the piston-engined C97. The American jet transport era began when the 367-80 first flew on 15 July 1954. Since then the aircraft has become probably the most modified in the world, in the course of developing and testing advanced features of later Boeing jet transports. 'Dash Eighty', the first American built jet transport, was accepted by the Smithsonian Institution as 'one of the 12 most significant aircraft of all time'.*

improvement on the earlier 120 series, with far better range and no water injection, though this facility was made available in later models for use on 'hot high' airfields (those airfields with high temperatures and high altitudes above sea level – both factors which adversely affected take-off). The Intercontinentals went into commercial service in August 1959. By that time there was a variety of 707s on the market, and the choice of type was to increase further with the introduction a few years later of the Boeing 707/320B (first ordered by Pan Am) with turbo-fan engines, giving a big improvement in fuel burn economy, and able to fly 20 per cent further than the 707/320, with the same payload. After the 320B came the 320C, convertible to full freighter, with the same turbo-fan engines as the 320B.

The Douglas DC8s were improved and developed over the same period, using the same type engines as the Boeing 707s, the DC8 turbo-fan aircraft being the 50 series.

Heavy reserves of fuel

Whereas the westbound wartime flying boats opted for the highest possible fuel reserves because of poor communications, scarcity of alternative airports, and 'busted' forecasts (which usually meant a headwind that had become stronger than forecast) the westbound jets of 20 or so years later also frequently carried higher than required reserves of fuel, but for different reasons. (Minimum reserves of fuel to be carried by an aircraft on a specific flight are spelt out in the Operations Manual, and must be approved by the relevant licensing authority.)

In early Atlantic jet flying it was sometimes possible that a westbound flight during peak departure time had to accept a flight level 4000 ft (1219 metres) lower than requested, because different airlines wanted the same 'best time–track'. Such a reduction in cruise level meant a dramatic increase in fuel to be burnt – on a typical Britain/America flight it could be as much as 4 per cent more.

It was sometimes desirable to carry fuel in excess of flight plan requirements (often referred to as stored fuel) provided it did not inhibit any weight limitation of the aircraft, for in addition to the penalty of failure to get requested flight level at peak departure times,

64 Boeing 707/120 – This was the logical successor to the 367-80 prototype, with similar lines, but larger and with higher maximum gross weight. The aircraft started commerical service with Pan American on 26 October 1958 on New York/Paris route.

65 The Boeing 707 Intercontinental *With more powerful engines, 3.65 metres (12 ft) greater wingspan, and 2.44 metres (8 ft) longer fuselage than the 707/120 series, this aircraft went into service over the longest routes in the world. This is the Rolls-Royce engined version of the Intercontinental, the 420 series as operated by BOAC. The Pratt & Whitney engined version was the 320 series.*

66 *An example of the Douglas DC8/30 series.*

67 An example of the Douglas DC8/50 series – *This was similarly engined to the Boeing 707/320B-320C series, with Pratt & Whitney turbo-fan powerplants.*

68 The Super VC10 – This stretched from the Standard model by 3.96 metres (13 ft). G-AGSA was the first of the type on North Atlantic routes on 1 April 1965.

69 DC8 jetliner production at Long Beach, California –
McDonnell Douglas Corporation produced three models of the DC8 to succeed the 50 series, the super 61 for transcontinental service, the super 62 for ultra-long range, and the super 63 for intercontinental routes. Both the super 61 and 63 were 11.8 metres (37 ft) longer than the standard DC8; the super 62 and 63 had greater wingspan and aerodynamic improvements. This was the final stretch of the famous Douglas DC8 line, with accommodation for over 250 passengers.

71 The DC8/61.

long holding could be experienced at the destination airport during peak arrival times, should there be a deterioration of terminal weather. New York International Airport often advised incoming flights of delays in landing of up to two hours, owing to weather deterioration; the actual holding time frequently turned out to be considerably less because those incoming flights with just basic reserves would, in view of the information from air traffic control, request an immediate clearance to an alternative airport, such as Boston or Washington. The lucky ones, with extra fuel reserves, would have sufficient fuel to hold for the originally estimated delay and then divert to another airport if necessary, before landing.

It was not, however, considered a good idea to carry fuel in excess of flight plan requirements for every trip for, as a jet aircraft gets lighter owing to fuel consumed, the rate of consumption of fuel per hour drops; and, conversely, if an aircraft is made heavier owing to extra payload or fuel, the rate of consumption of fuel rises. Therefore if, say, 5000 kg (11,000 lb) of fuel were added for extra contingency to early jets over an Atlantic sector, about 20 to 25 per cent of that extra fuel would have been burnt in order to carry it. In certain circumstances, the practice of loading stored fuel provided cheap insurance against possible diversion to an alternative airport.

North Atlantic tracks

The introduction of North Atlantic tracks (NAT), with vertical and lateral separation control, did much to regularize and aid Atlantic jet flying. The tracks, identified by code letter, were issued twice a day, based on favourable time-tracks for east and westbound traffic, giving ocean co-ordinates and entry and exit points for each track. Flight levels allocated for use within track structure allowed for optimum use of available airspace.

Over and under the low

It will be apparent from television and newspaper weather maps displaying isobars (lines joining points of equal pressure) that in the northern hemisphere the wind flows anticlockwise around a low pressure system, and clockwise around a high pressure system (in the southern hemisphere the reverse holds good). A feature of North Atlantic jet flying is that eastbound and westbound aircraft flying from and to the same airports, at around the same time, can be hundreds of miles apart, each one making full use of the pressure pattern to achieve the best time-track. The westbound aircraft, flying north of a deep low, though increasing distance, can pick up some tailwinds, while the eastbound aircraft, planned south of the same low, also increasing distance, will also pick up tailwinds to achieve the best time-track.

72 Shannon Airport − Introduction
of the stretched Douglas DC8 −
especially the DC8/61 which was
short of range for transatlantic
operation − by many American based
charter airlines in the late 1960s was a
boon for Shannon, strategically placed
as a fuel stop for the heavily laden
America/Europe/America charter
traffic. By 1969 transit passengers were
back to the late fifties peak and
terminal traffic was growing rapidly.

Chapter 5 1970 on:

The wide bodies, the supersonics and the future

Transatlantic wide-bodied and supersonic jets

The Boeing 747 introduced completely new concepts in airline passenger accommodation with a capability of carrying 550 passengers. The sheer volume of the aircraft also made possible a revolution in high-speed air transportation of outsize cargo, hitherto impossible to carry. With the coming of the 747, loads were trebled and airports strained, but one great bonus existed for the world's international airports – because of the highly developed wing-flap system and a 16-wheel four-main-truck landing gear, the 747 needed runways no longer than those used by existing narrow bodied jets, such as the DC8 and the B707.

As more powerful engines became available, pushing the 747's maximum structural take-off weight to over 376,500 kg (830,000 lb), new range and load capabilities were possible. By 1975, seven different models were available, the seventh being the 747SP – the 'SP' standing for special performance. With the 747, the wide-bodied tri-jets, the DC10 and the Lockheed Tristar also progressed in range and load capacity, as new technology engines provided improved thrust and better fuel consumption.

Supersonic (faster than the speed of sound) transatlantic flights to New York were initiated on 19 October 1977, and regular passenger service began on 22 November when an Air France Concorde landed at New York International/JFK two minutes ahead of a British Airways Concorde which took off simultaneously. The Air France flight had originated at Paris, and the BA flight at London/Heathrow. Both British Airways and Air France Concordes had been operating scheduled services from London and Paris respectively to Washington, DC for 18 months before regular flights to New York started.

73 An Air Canada Lockheed Tristar takes off from Heathrow.

The Atlantic bargain basement

Much has been achieved in recent years in aviation: better air traffic control, vast improvements in navigation systems, fewer diversions from destination airports and standardization of flying techniques. From the passengers' point of view, the most important aspect of Atlantic flying has been the bargain fares – stemming from Pan Am's battle for tourist fares in the 1950s – available in the comfort and safety of the modern wide-bodied fan-jets. To appreciate the sheer value of Atlantic fares, comparison should be made, on a mile for mile basis,

with 1987 European scheduled fares. A spot check comparing London/Paris and London/New York using great circle (shortest possible) distances for both sectors revealed London/Paris (215 st miles, 345 km) one-way economy fare was £75 and London/New York (3440 st miles, 5536 km) cheapest one-way economy fare was £199. On a mile for mile basis the London/Paris sector is six times more expensive.

Range of aircraft has long since ceased to be a problem, and flying the Alantic no longer means just flying from London to New York or Montreal. Today, flying the Atlantic means, for Europeans, holidays in Florida, the Caribbean and the Pacific coast; for Americans it means holidays anywhere in Europe, the Middle East, North Africa. All holiday-makers, whether east or westbound, enjoy the multitude of special fares and package tours, which are so much part of the prestige Atlantic routes.

74 A McDonnell Douglas DC10-40 — (the first in Northwest markings) takes off from Long Beach Municipal Airport, beside the Douglas Aircraft Company division of McDonnell Douglas. Easy identification of the two successful tri-jets, Tristar and DC10, is provided by the rear engines in each type — on the Tristar range the engine blends into the fuselage, while the DC10's rear engine is located mid-tail.

75 Busy day for Pan Am at Heathrow's cargo centre (left) – *The 160-acre cargo terminal is Britain's busiest air freight despatch and accepting point. Special attractions of the terminal are its convenient situation and motorway link.*

North Atlantic trends

A further derivative of the Boeing 747 will appear on world routes by the end of 1988. This will be the 747/400. The new 400 series will have yet greater range than existing models, plus much improved fuel economy. Range capability should embrace London/Honolulu non-stop with a full passenger load. The long range twin engined fan-jets, such as the Boeing 767/200ER (ER for extended range), currently used on some Atlantic routes, are likely to be used more extensively.

76 Heathrow (above) – *tails of many operators.*

77 A five-engined 747 – A not uncommon sight, which often goes unnoticed by passengers. This 747, equipped with a fifth engine between the inboard engine and the left side of the fuselage, is shown taking off from Boeing Field, Seattle, on one of the flight tests leading to certification of the 747 to carry a spare engine in commercial service when necessary. Fifth engines are replacement powerplants being carried to points on airline routes where needed, or being returned to the airline base. The engine, enclosed in a pod similar to the regular engine, has the blades of the turbofan section at the front of the engine removed for shipment. With the fifth engine installed, cruise speed is slightly less than standard. Boeing 707s also had provision for carrying podded spare engines.

78 A Concorde at Gander International Airport – *British Airways used Gander International for Concorde training. There were four development aircraft, two prototypes being 001 and 002, and two pre-production aircraft, labelled 01 and 02. F-WTSA was 02, the second pre-production aircraft. This French-assembled aircraft first flew in January 1973.*

79 Dorval Airport, Montreal 1979
– In November 1975 the new
Montreal International Airport opened
at Mirabel, and all the overseas flight
operations were transferred to Mirabel
from Dorval. Since 1975 Dorval has
been providing domestic air services
within Canada, and transborder
services to various destinations in the
USA. Whatever its present status as
an airport, Dorval has carved its
special place in the history of Atlantic
flying.

80 747/400 – *The 747/400 will be a familiar sight on Atlantic routes in the late 1980s and 1990s.*

81 Long range Atlantic twin engined contender – *The Boeing 767/200ER (ER = Extended Range).*

The hypersonic revolution to come

By far the most exciting prospect for future Atlantic flight is what is termed hypersonic flight — mach 5 (five times the speed of sound), or faster. That remarkable gentleman, the late Sir Barnes Wallis, is said to have commented that we should never have wasted time and money on the Concorde project, but should have concentrated on hypersonic flight, in the area of mach 10 (ten times the speed of sound) capable of London/Sydney non-stop in an hour or so. It is understood that Sir Barnes went on to say that the technology was there, and all that was needed was the money. He was right about many things, and could well have been right about this.

One possibility for the future is the British HOTOL (horizontal take-off and landing), British Aerospace's concept for a mach 5 satellite-delivery system, based on a horizontal take-off and landing vehicle, operating from conventional airports. In America the green light has been given, and vast sums of money made available, for the development of the aerospaceplane by the year 2000. Boeing, Lockheed, McDonnell Douglas and others have revealed their concepts for trans-atmospheric vehicles.

The space vehicle will surely come, but who knows when, what its speed will be and what means of propulsion will be used, or indeed who will design and build it. If asked to wager a guess, I would never discount the partnership of Boeing and Pan American which began with the 314 flying boat back in the 1930s, and continued with the B377 Stratocruiser, the B707 and the B747.

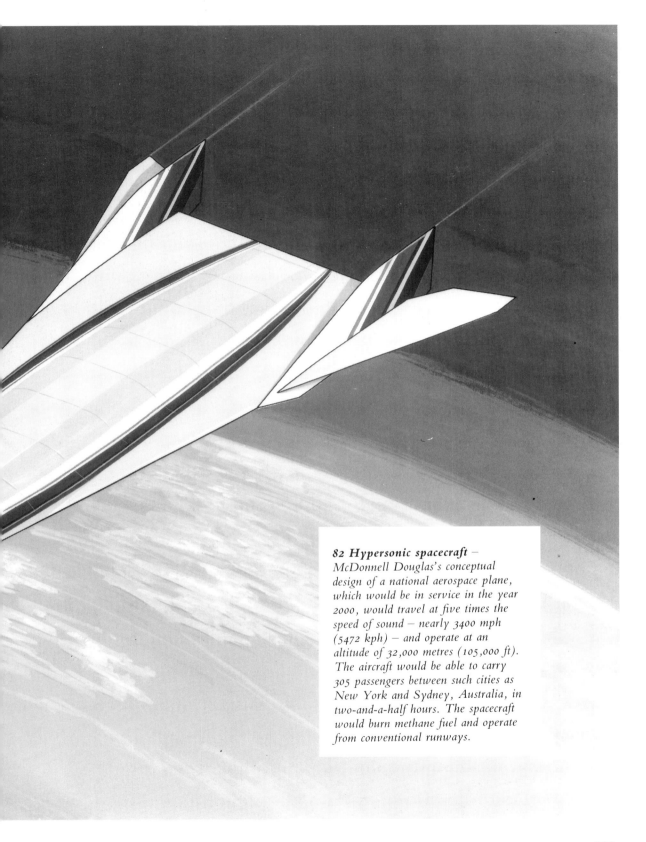

82 Hypersonic spacecraft –
McDonnell Douglas's conceptual
design of a national aerospace plane,
which would be in service in the year
2000, would travel at five times the
speed of sound – nearly 3400 mph
(5472 kph) – and operate at an
altitude of 32,000 metres (105,000 ft).
The aircraft would be able to carry
305 passengers between such cities as
New York and Sydney, Australia, in
two-and-a-half hours. The spacecraft
would burn methane fuel and operate
from conventional runways.

Appendix – Glossary of terms

Airway A control area or portion thereof established in the form of a corridor equipped with radio navigational aids.

Best time-track See Track.

Control area A controlled airspace extending upwards from a specified height above the surface of the earth without an upper limit unless one is stated.

Cross wind Side winds affecting an aircraft on take-off or landing.

Fuel burn-off Fuel consumed from take-off to touch down.

Fuel reserves Total fuel on board at take-off less fuel burn-off.

Fuel stored Total fuel reserves less required reserves for a specific sector.

GCA (Ground Controlled Approach) A landing aid using radar to talk down aircraft in poor weather conditions.

Hypersonic See mach number.

Mach number The ratio of true airspeed to the speed of sound. Mach number = TAS (true airspeed) divided by the speed of sound. Subsonic aircraft will have a mach number of less than one (modern long range jets cruise in the region of mach 0.82/0.86). Supersonic aircraft will cruise at more than mach one, where supersonic flight is permitted. The term 'hypersonic' is applied to aircraft with a mach number of five or higher. The speed of sound varies with height and with temperature at a given height.

NAT (North Atlantic Tracks) See Track.

Payload The load carried that produces revenue: the weight of passengers and their baggage, mail and freight, carried on the aircraft.

PNR (point of no return) A point plotted on a flight plan, based on endurance and forecast upper winds. Up to this point an aircraft may return to its airport of departure with pre-planned reserves of fuel on arrival there.

Pressurisation Normal atmospheric pressure maintained in aircraft cabin at altitude.

Runway limited Limitation imposed on an aircraft, owing to runway length, to reach its maximum take-off weight, or a sufficiently high take-off weight, to complete a sector with booked payload and required sector fuel.

Subsonic See mach number.

Supersonic See mach number.

TAS (True Air Speed) The speed of an aircraft relative to undisturbed air.

Track The projection on the earth's surface of the path of an aircraft – usually expressed as latitude/longitude over an ocean segment.

Best time-track – the track providing the fastest possible time from airport to airport, based on upper winds, and not necessarily the shortest distance.

NAT (North Atlantic Tracks) – organized tracks, formulated and published twice daily, the disposition of each track governed by, mainly, the forecast meteorological situation. Operators may opt for the most suitable track for the sector concerned and choose a flight level from those allocated within the track structure.

'*Wet lease*' Leasing contract of an aircraft, usually between two airlines, by which the lessor also provides sufficient operating crews to fly the aircraft and maintenance facility to cover scheduled and unscheduled maintenance over the specific period (the crews may or may not include cabin crews). The lessee will be responsible for all handling, landing and navigation charges and fuel costs for the lease period.

Wet take-off The use of a water injection facility for take-off.

Bibliography

Anonymous. *Aviation on the Shannon*. Irish Air Letter. 25 Phoenix Avenue, Castleknock, Dublin 15, Ireland, 1985.

Arend, G. *Great airports – Kennedy International*. Air Cargo News Inc. 1985.

Atlantic Bridge. HMSO. (Prepared for the Ministry of Information.) 1945.

Beaty, D. *The water jump*. Secker and Warburg, 1977.

Boeing Airplane Company. *Pedigree of Champions*. 1984.

Ewart, J. *Prestwick Airport, golden jubilee. 1935–85*.

Munson, K. *Airlines since 1946*. Blandford Press, 1975.